I'M TRYING to Love GeRMS

WORDS & PICTURES by
bethany bARTon

VIKING

STAPHYLOCOCCUS EPIDERMIDIS
"staff-low-kah-cuss epp-eh-derm-uh-diss"
common bacteria that
live on human skin

THIS BOOK IS COVERED IN GERMS!

BUT TO BE FAIR, SO ARE YOU. INSIDE AND OUT.

ASPERGILLUS NIGER
"as-per-gill-lus ny-jer"
a fungus commonly found
on food—causes mold to
grow on damp fruits & veggies

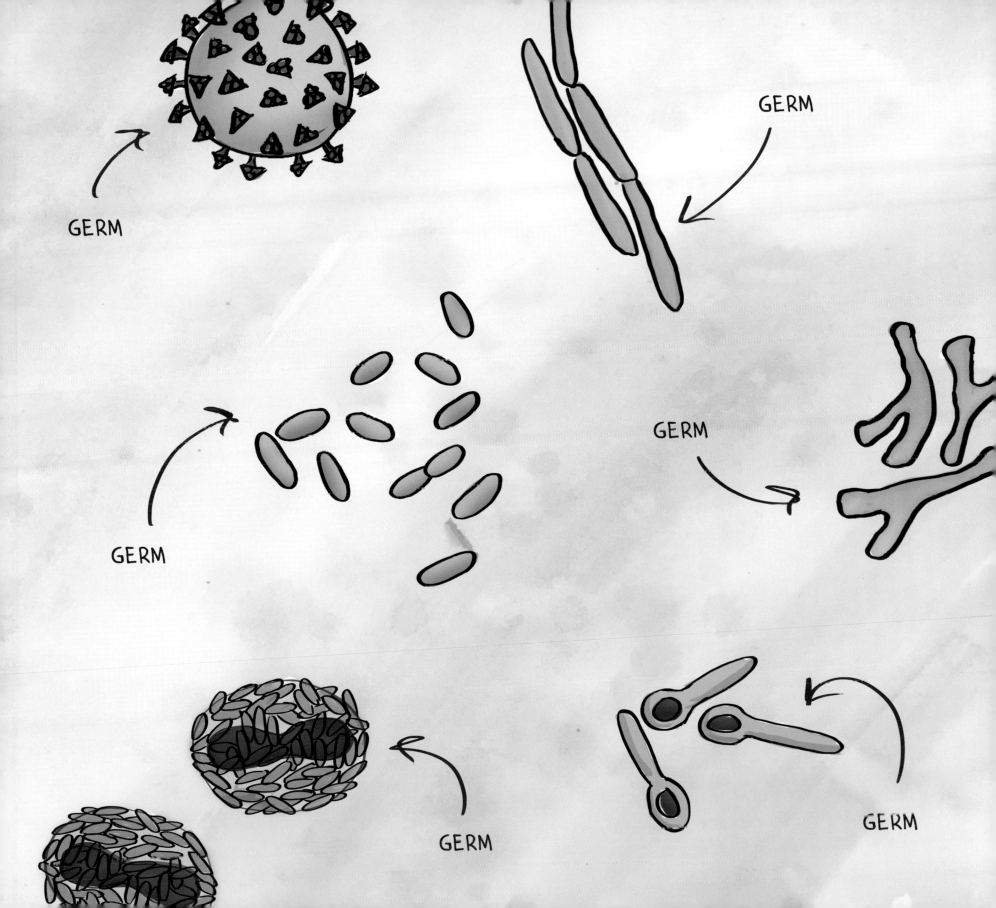

For Mike and Leo: my favorites. I love you lots.

Also for every teacher, librarian, or educator who has ever
shared a book with a curious mind. Y'all are my heroes.

Big thanks to my smart, inspiring siblings (who aren't scared of germs):
Dr. Bridget Hurry, MD (Bridy), Jessica Ressa, MPT (Jesse), and Graham Hogan, MS (Gramo)

Extra-big thanks to Dr. Erik Mogalian, PharmD, PhD,
for lending his impressive knowledge and fact-checking these germy pages
(during a pandemic . . . while he was super busy with immunology stuff . . . I'm super grateful!)

Also to Anne Roubal, PhD, for checking out my endpapers (and doing cool work with germs!)

VIKING
An imprint of Penguin Random House LLC, New York

First published in the United States of America by Viking, an imprint of Penguin Random House LLC, 2023

Copyright © 2023 by Bethany Barton

Visit us online at PenguinRandomHouse.com.

LIBRARY OF CONGRESS CATALOGING-IN-PUBLICATION DATA IS AVAILABLE.

Manufactured in China

ISBN 9780593326725

1 3 5 7 9 10 8 6 4 2

TOPL

The artwork in this book was created using ink and Beam Handmade Watercolor paints (which are sustainable
and altogether rad) on paper, alongside Photoshop CC. The main text was lettered with a well-loved bamboo
calligraphy pen and ink. Innumerable cups of tea were consumed in the process.

YOU CAN'T EVEN SEE
the GERMS ON THIS BOOK.

THEY'RE **THAT** SMALL.

CAN'T-BE-SEEN-WITH-
YOUR-REGULAR-EYEBALLS SMALL.

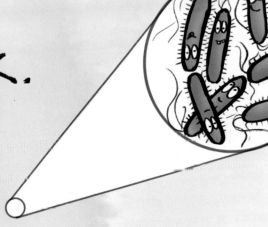

PROTEUS MIRABILIS
"pro-tee-us mer-ab-uh-luss"
bacteria found in human
& animal intestines

NEISSERIA
"nice-sear-ria"
genus of bacteria found
in the upper respiratory
tracts of humans & animals

Can't be
pronounced either!

WAIT. WHO SAID THAT?
It's me! Over here!
I CAN'T REALLY SEE YOU. ARE YOU A TALKING GERM?
I sure am!

THANKFULLY THIS BOOK HAS the LATEST IN

ZOOMY-INNY TECHNOLOGY™

VERY ADVANCED STUFF.

HERE, READER FRIENDS: JUST MOVE YOUR THUMB AND INDEX FINGER AWAY FROM EACH OTHER to ZOOM IN CLOSER.

TOO CLOSE. THI

S IS TOO CLOSE.

PINCH IN
to ZOOM OUT.

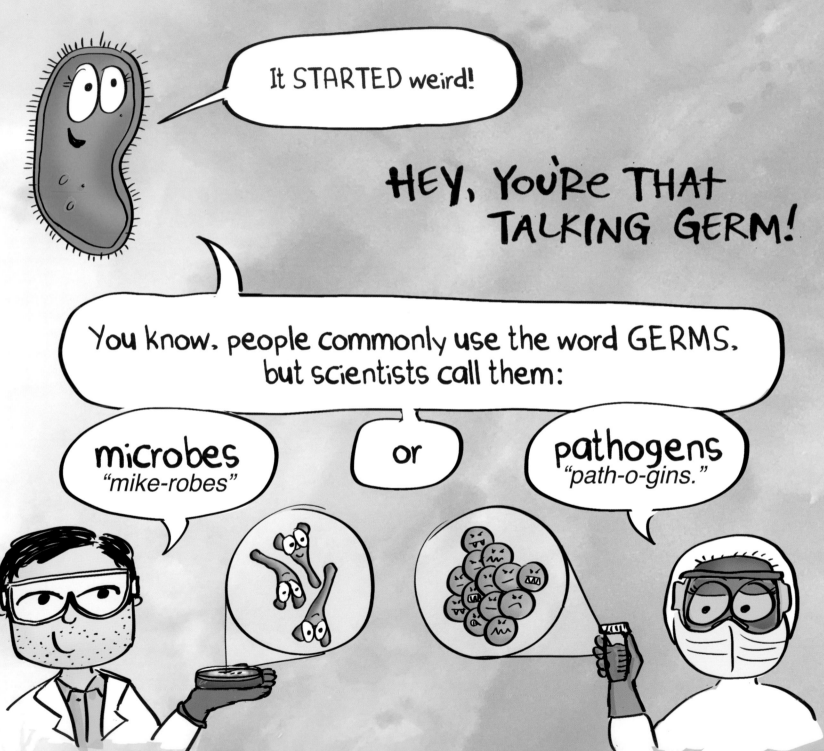

Microbes are microscopic organisms

"my-crow-ska-pic or-gan-iz-ums,"

which just means teeny-tiny living things.

So I'm more of a microbe really.
But you can call me a
talking germ if you want.

UM. OKAY. WELL, I'M TRYING TO LOVE GERMS. COULD YOU HELP ME WITH THAT?

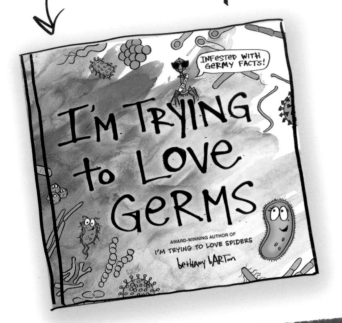

That's weird. Why would you want to do that?

Did you mean to say MICROBES?

Microbes are neither good nor bad. Kinda like humans.

They can be helpful or harmful.

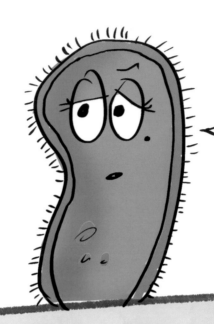

Aspergillus niger
"as-per-gill-lus ny-jer"

Neisseria
"nice-sear-ria"

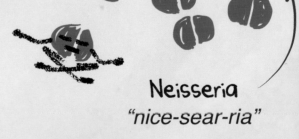

But when people say GERMS,
they're usually talking about PATHOGENS.
Pathogens are the microbes that make you sick.

Pathogens cause stuff like

barfing,   sneezing,   and diarrhea!

So pathogens are no fun.

But most microbes are great. (Like me.)

Humans (like you) actually have billions of helpful microbes in their bodies, doing important stuff you need to survive.

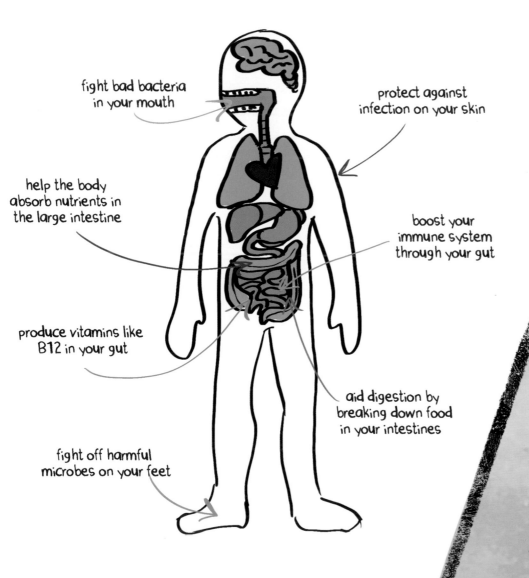

fight bad bacteria in your mouth

protect against infection on your skin

help the body absorb nutrients in the large intestine

boost your immune system through your gut

produce vitamins like B12 in your gut

aid digestion by breaking down food in your intestines

fight off harmful microbes on your feet

It's been said humans host ten microorganisms (that's a big word for microbes) for every single cell in their bodies.

So technically . . . you're Trying to Love Microbes.

But the Book is already printed.
I can't change it now.

So... Is there Anything Lovable About Germs?

Okay, I happen to think germs, even the gross ones, are pretty fascinating.

Scientists debate if viruses should even be called "alive," making them almost like zombies!

...brains...

And sometimes just appreciating how different something is can make you love it!

SOUNDS LIKE A PLAN. WHERE DO WE START?

Let me introduce you to some of my favorite little troublemakers: the four most famous types of pathogens.

bacterium

virus

fungus

protozoan

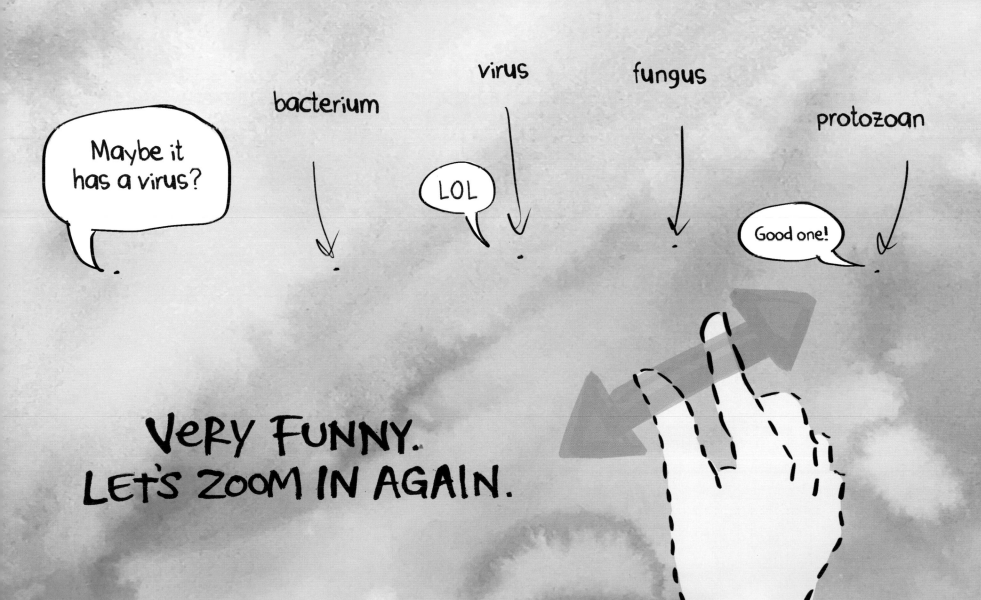

OH. WOW. I'M NOT SURE WHAT I WAS EXPECTING, BUT THIS... WAS NOT IT.

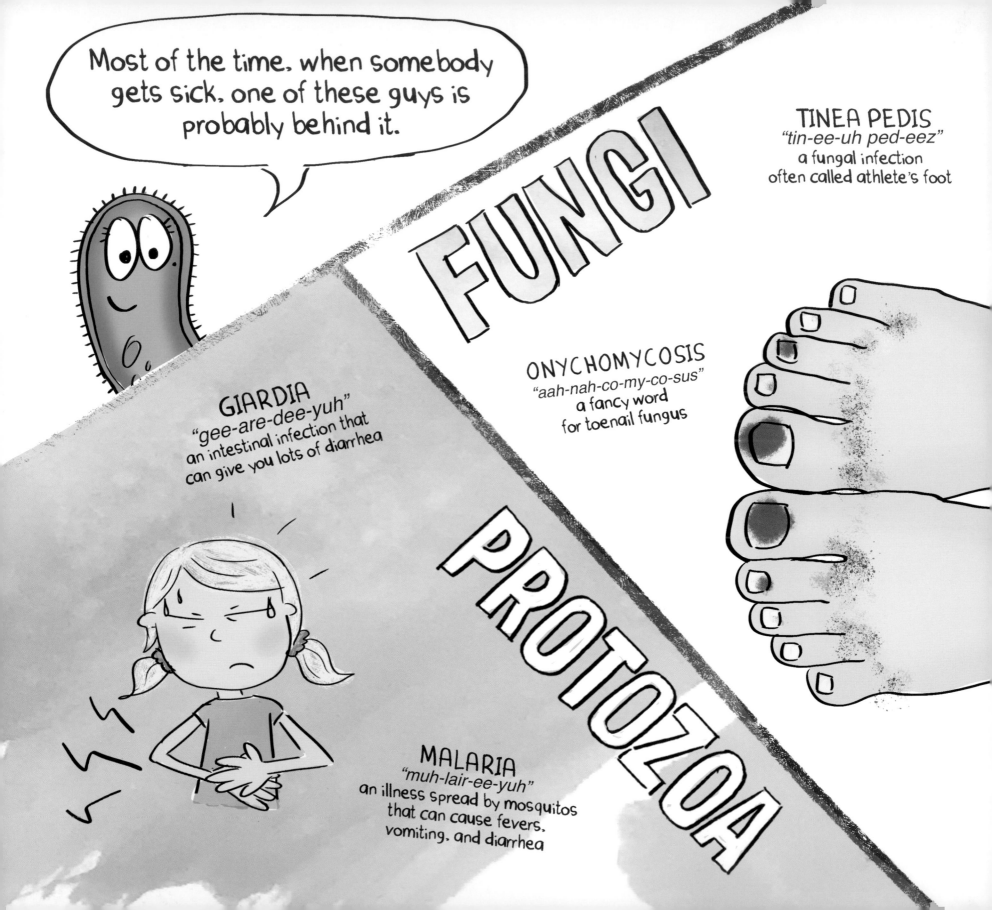

BACTERIA

STREPTOCOCCUS
"strep-tuh-kah-cuss"
a group of bacteria responsible
for painful sore throats
(commonly called strep throat)

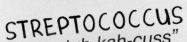

ESCHERICHIA COLI
(aka E. COLI)
"esh-er-rick-ee-yuh cole-lie"
a bacteria known to cause
food-borne illness
(commonly called
food poisoning)

RHINOVIRUS
"rhy-no-vai-russ"
a virus that causes
the common cold

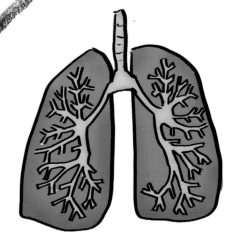

CORONAVIRUS
"core-oh-nuh-vai-russ"
a family of viruses that
cause respiratory tract illness

VIRUSES

FUNGI

PENICILLIUM
"pen-uh-sill-ee-um"
a fungi used to make penicillin, an antibiotic that has saved millions of lives

AGARICUS BISPORUS
"uh-gare-ick-cuss bih-spore-us"
commonly called cremini mushrooms, these make a great pizza topping

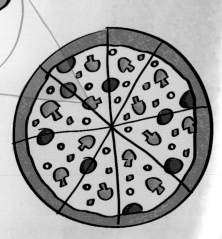

LACTOCOCCUS LACTIS
"lack-tuh-kah-cuss lack-tuhs"
a bacteria used to make yogurt and cheese

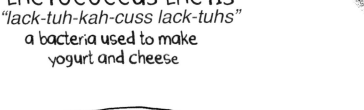

BACTEROIDETES
"back-tur-royd-et-tees"
these hang out in your gut and help you digest food

BACTERIA

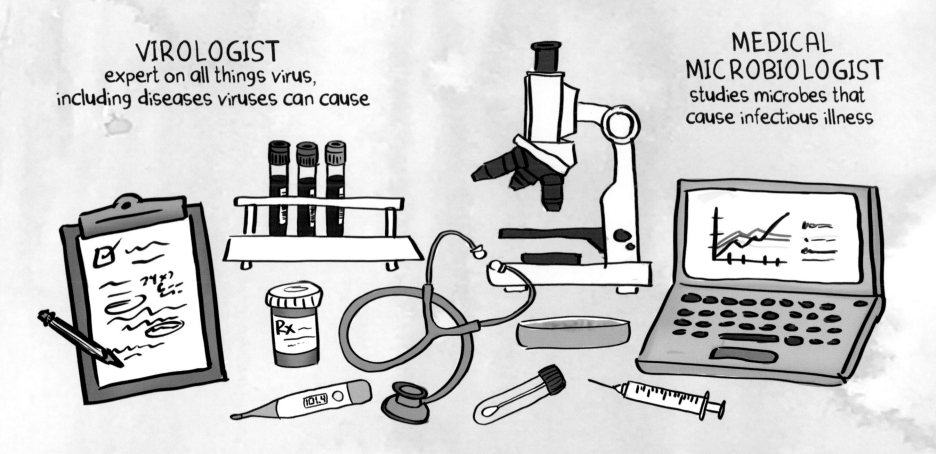

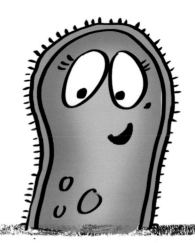

That's right! For some people, learning about pathogens and helping people is so important, they find a way to make it happen.

Just like you wear a bike helmet and follow traffic rules, they use safety gear and follow guidelines to help them interact safely with infectious germs.

WHOA. THEY MUST REALLY LOVE GERMS.
I DON'T LOVE GERMS. NOT YET.
BUT I AM STARTING TO APPRECIATE
HOW WEIRD THEY ARE.

AND I REALLY DON'T WANT to GET SICK.

SO HOW DO I AVOID ALL THE DISEASE-CAUSING PATHOGENS?

WHOA! WHERE'D YOU ALL GO?

We're still here!

We're teeny-tiny, remember?

Which is why the first step for avoiding pathogens is avoiding contact with the places they love to hide.

sick people

coughs & sneezes

boogers

germy stuff

Sometimes contact is unavoidable. Doctors and nurses touch lots of germs! That's why many wear masks and gloves to keep from sharing or spreading pathogens.

Germs still made contact? Fear not! These heroes break down the cell walls of most germs—destroying them before they can infect you.

While your body is super-skilled at fighting off pathogens, sometimes it needs a little help.

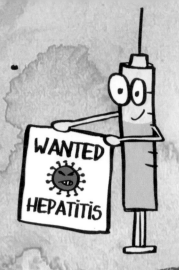

VACCINES help give your body instructions on how to destroy specific pathogens so it can attack them right away— sometimes before you even feel sick!

MEDICINES can also attack germs, or help keep them from multiplying.

ANTIVIRALS help slow down viral infections

(like the flu).

ANTIFUNGALS target harmful fungal infections

(like toenail fungus).

ANITIBIOTICS go after troublesome bacteria

(like the ones that cause earaches).

Now **THAT'S** something I can love: stopping pathogens from ruining my day.

Thanks for the help, germy friends!

HIGH-FIVE!

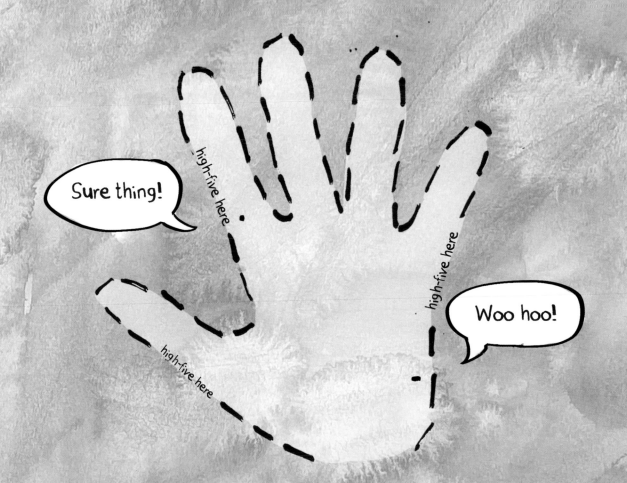

WHOOPS.

I'M COVERED IN THOSE GERMS NOW, AREN'T I?

I would wash my hands if I were you.

A Word on Washing Your Hands

Can't get enough of germs?
Check out these awesome resources!

You already know how to save lives, and you do it with a skill you probably don't think much about: washing your hands.

I like to think of germs like glitter. Imagine if when you coughed or sneezed, a whole bunch of glitter came out. You'd have glitter on your hands, your arms, probably on your shirt too. You know how glitter tends to get everywhere and stick to everything? Germs do kind of the same thing. They love to travel, often hitching a ride on our hands and looking for a new place to call home (or body to infect). Thankfully, we can wash our hands to keep from spreading troublesome microbes to others.

Salmonella typhi, for example, is a bacteria that can hang out in poop and causes a dangerous illness called typhoid. In the early 1900s, a cook now famously referred to as Typhoid Mary didn't know she was a carrier of Salmonella typhi and infected dozens of people with typhoid. A few people even died. Mary was interviewed and admitted she almost never washed her hands. This wasn't unusual back then—people didn't know a lot about germs and how they traveled. But it also meant that she was spreading the disease by not washing her hands very well (if at all) after using the bathroom or before handling food . . . blech!

Thankfully we know better now. You can help save lives by using that very simple superpower: washing your hands. Just make sure you do it for twenty seconds or more (about as long as it takes to sing the "Happy Birthday" song twice) with soap and water. Germs won't stand a chance!

Here are some resources for more learning! I read A LOT, and these were my very favorites:

It's Catching: The Infectious World of Germs and Microbes by Jennifer Gardy, PhD, illustrated by Josh Holinaty (Jennifer Gardy, if you're reading this: I love your book; please be my best friend.)

Up Your Nose by Seth Fishman, illustrated by Isabel Greenberg (Seth Fishman, if you're reading this: I love your book, and thanks for being my friend.)

The Bacteria Book: The Big World of Really Tiny Microbes by Steve Mould

Germy Science: The Sick Truth about Getting Sick (and Staying Healthy) by Edward Kay, illustrated by Mike Shiell

All in a Drop: How Antony van Leeuwenhoek Discovered an Invisible World by Lori Alexander, illustrated by Vivien Mildenberger

Inside your Insides: A Guide to the Microbes That Call You Home by Claire Eamer, illustrated by Marie-Ève Tremblay

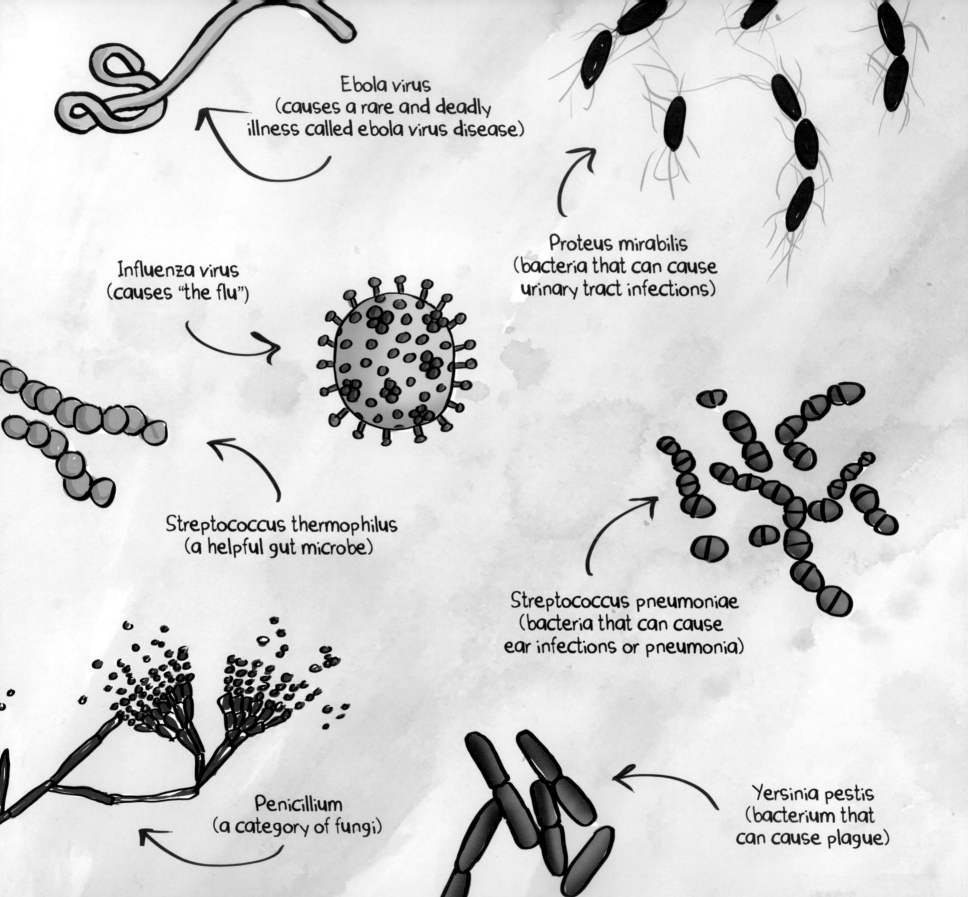

Ebola virus
(causes a rare and deadly
illness called ebola virus disease)

Proteus mirabilis
(bacteria that can cause
urinary tract infections)

Influenza virus
(causes "the flu")

Streptococcus thermophilus
(a helpful gut microbe)

Streptococcus pneumoniae
(bacteria that can cause
ear infections or pneumonia)

Penicillium
(a category of fungi)

Yersinia pestis
(bacterium that
can cause plague)